Life Lessons

Or, I Wish I Knew Then, What I Know Now

by

Joe Poyer

North Cape Publications, Inc.

This booklet is for my grandchildren —

**Kelsey, Kassandra, Tyler, and Kylie Poyer,
and
Abrielle Paige Jasman**

— in hopes that some of the life lessons I have
learned in 76-plus years will be of benefit to them.

ISBN 978-1-882391-51-6
North Cape Publications®, Inc.,
P.O. Box 1027, Tustin, CA 92781
Email: ncape@ix.netcom.com

Kelsy Nicole Poyer

Tyler Joseph Poyer

Kassandra Michelle Poyer

Kylie Marie Poyer

Abrielle Paige Jasman

You live only once, but if you do it right, once is enough.

Mae West

Life Lessons
Or, I Wish I Knew Then,
What I know Now

The following pages include rules, or perhaps truisms, that I have learned the hard way over some seventy-plus years of life. If I had known about them earlier, I might have avoided many mistakes. Some that are included in the following pages you may think trite. And some, you may snicker at now, but wonder why you did so when you are in your 50's and 60's. In any event, I hope these few pages will help you navigate your life.

Basic Truisms

It's the Things You Don't Know That Can Hurt You.

Every Decision You Will Make Will Have Unexpected and/or Unintended Consequences.

You Are the Center of Your Universe. But Not the Center of Anyone Else's.
Seven billion plus (at present) people are also claiming to be the centers of the universe.

Life Is Not Fair. Do Not Expect It To Be.
The universe is ignorant of your existence.

Life Goes By Too Fast.
Make the most of every day. Try and do something you have never done before. Try to learn something new every day.

What Doesn't Kill You, Makes You Stronger.
You will fail at any number of things in life. Use the failures as learning lessons — what did YOU do wrong and how can YOU do better next time.

Whatever Task You Undertake, Do Your Best.
Dr. Martin Luther King said, "If life makes you a street sweeper, be the best street sweeper you can be."

Your First Reactions To Any New Idea or Process Will Be To Dismiss It; Resist The Urge.
Avoid the NIH (Not Invented Here) syndrome. Consider carefully before making up your mind.

Do Not Always Listen To What Other People Say.
Most of what I learned about life from my friends or peers before I was thirty-five was wrong or incomplete. Much of what I

learned after thirty-five from my friends or peers had to be taken with a grain of salt. Do your own research.

Use Your Common Sense.
Common sense is built on what you should have learned after doing the wrong thing.

Develop Problem Solving Skills
Your parents won't always be around to bail you out, nor should they. They have problems of their own. If you have a problem, do not react emotionally; stop and think about how best to work around it. Then do it even if it takes several tries.

Don't Ignore "Old" People. They Have A Lifetime of Experience To Impart.
Why learn the hard way what they already have?

Advice
Listen carefully to any you are given, then decide if you want to follow it. Don't give advice unless the recipient really, really asks you for it. They probably won't follow it anyway and so you are just wasting your time.

Luck
"Thorough preparation is its own best luck."
(Stole that from one of my own novels)

Follow The Golden Rule
Do unto others as you would have them do unto you – but do not be disappointed when they do not. It's still a good way to live.

Planning Your Life, Or Just The Next Day
Serendipity will change your life more than anything you plan. Remember the old Yiddish proverb: *Der mentsh trakht un Got lakht.* (Man plans, God laughs).

There are three types of people in this world

Predators

Victims

Wary

Be the latter

Companies

Seven Rules:

1. Corporations are "persons" but without souls, emotions, or gratitude.

2. All corporate objectives are — in order — maximize profits, accumulate market share (power), and survive. Nothing else matters to a corporation.

3. Do not trust anything a corporation, or its employees, tell you about your chance for advancement, or the quality of its products. The first consideration is always corporate growth and their personal advancement.

4. When a company says you are "part of the team," remember two things:

> First, top-level executive management is not a part of that team. They have their own goals and loyalties and they rarely include you as an employee.

> Secondly, teams eliminate teammates for a variety of reasons, and those reasons are never in your best interest.

5. The only thing a company owes you is your salary. Do not expect loyalty. The only thing you owe a company is a fair day's work.

6. When you work for another, you do not receive what you deserve; you receive what you negotiate.

7. Never contact a working person on Monday with a problem if you can help it; wait until Tuesday.

Why? People are starting their work week on Monday, trying to get organized and fighting fires that cropped up over the weekend and they will give you short shrift if you bother them at this time.

By Tuesday, most fires are out and things are running better. They are more liable to give you their full attention then.

Day Dreaming

Contrary to what many think, day dreaming is a very important contribution to both your mental health and creativity.

It is a way to take your mind off day-to-day cares and problems for short periods. It also allows your mind to free-associate and that often provides not only new ideas, but new ways of thinking about things.

Set aside a few moments periodically during the day to let your mind wander. Most importantly, encourage children to day dream as well.

Encourage them to dream about becoming super heroes, cowboys, astronauts, writers, or brilliant scientists, etc.

Dress and Comportment

Men should always wear a suit to weddings, funerals, award ceremonies, interviews and other formal occassions. It shows respect for others, and for yourself.

Women should never wear mini-skirts to funerals. It shows disrespect for the deceased and family. Only wear a mini- or short-skirt to a wedding if you are not competing with the bride. The same for award ceremonies. For business interviews, dress modestly and in a businesslike manner. Those who will interview you will be more interested in your mind and ability to do the job, than your looks.

Men and Women should always wear well-polished shoes for business or other formal occasions. People do judge you by your appearance.

Men should never wear a baseball cap backwards unless you are the catcher in a baseball game. Adults will think you are too dumb to know whether you are coming or going. The bill on the cap was invented to shade your eyes from the sun, not to look "cool."

Sometime you will have to do, attend, or perform an activity you dislike. Go and make the best of it. You will gratify friends and family and will probably learn or derive something useful.

When speaking on the phone, speak up and do not mumble. The person on the other end will think that you are intelligent and confident.

At the end of the phone conversation, do not drop your voice or let it trail away. That shows disrespect for the person on the other end and implies the conversation was not important.

Do not let your life be controlled by those in power. Question whatever they tell you until you are satisfied that you want to do it what they want. If not, find a way to say no.

If you drink alcohol, do so carefully, and never allow yourself to become drunk, in private or public. Alcohol modifies the part of the brain that controls behavior. Besides the hangover, you may have far more to regret the next day as too many predators are waiting to take advantage of you and will.

Avoid the siren call of drugs. A drug habit *always* ends your life badly.

Friends

Friends are important to your well-being. But be careful of whom you befriend.

Choose your friends not for convenience — they live near, you take the same classes, work in the same place, are always available — but for shared interests, personality, and generosity.

Make certain that they are someone you genuinely like.

Avoid "friends" who are demanding, push you to do things you do not want to do, insist of vetting your other friends, and criticize you. This type of friend is toxic and will turn on you sooner or later.

Government

1. Government is not your friend — it is your servant. Do not let it treat *you* as the servant.

2. Government, by its very nature, is composed of a series of bureaucracies, and bureaucracies, by their very nature, will seek to extend their power, which means power over you. Doing the job they were formed to do comes a long way second.

3. Government does not have your best interest at heart. To government at any level, you are just another cog in the wheel that powers their mission to extend their influence and power.

4. To control your governments in the United States of America — municipal, county, state, and federal — keep abreast of what they arc doing through your local media, especially the newspapers, then vote. But recognize that the media are 1) driven by advertising dollars, 2) require access to politicians, and 3) their news will often be slanted against your interests.

Also, publishers, editors, and reporters have their own political, moral, and religious outlooks.

5. Compromise is the essence of good government. No one should ever expect to get everything they want, all the time. Stalin, Hitler, Mussolini, Pol Pot never once considered compromise as a way to govern. Any politician who refuses to compromise, as a matter of principal, should be ejected by the voters.

6. Vote in every election. Your vote counts. John F. Kennedy won the Presidency by an average of one vote in every precinct.

Prepare yourself by studying the issues. Too many voters are swayed by a candidate's popularity with minority elements of the voters (tea party, progressives, etc.). Don't you be.

7. Candidates with radical objectives are dangerous. Good government results from compromise.

6. "Political outsiders" rarely make good governors, presidents, or prime ministers. By the time they learn how to navigate the political system, their term is up or they are thrown out of office.

Media

Television news, both local and network, as currently consti-
tuted, is almost useless for factual reporting. Most of the "news"
networks and virtually all of the large metropolitan and national
newspapers have political agendas.

They are also driven by audience ratings which are largely pro-
duced by crime and scandal stories, none of which are investi-
gated in any depth. The old journalistic truism — "If it bleeds, it
leads" — drives news reporting today. Ignore most of what they
tell you.

Networks as well as most local television channels and radio sta-
tions rarely have budgets for full-time investigative staff reporters.

Even worse are most internet **blogs**. The blog concept developed
on the internet to allow individuals to express their personal opin-
ions. The vast majority of bloggers write from emotion and not
facts. Why would you be swayed by someone else's emotional
outbursts?

Many **blogs** that publish periodically are written in a sensational-
ist manner to increase their viewership. Most of the "news" they
present is poorly researched, if at all.

Actors and celebrities often espouse philosophical and political views and are used by spokespersons for political and social causes.

Actors: If successful, they make a living portraying fictional people. Most have little or no education beyond high school or a few years of drama instruction. They live in a bubble of adulation and money. Why would you be swayed by anything they say or believe?

Celebrities: Those who are not actors become famous for some silly act that garnered media attention. They are adept at maintaining that media interest. Again, why would you be swayed by anything they say or believe?

Interviewing For a Job

Accepting a job can be one of the most important influences in your life, particularly if it is not one in line with your anticipated career. You may take a job as a temporary measure until you find your career path, but then wonder years later while still in the same job, how you allowed yourself to give up your dreams. If you are educated, personable, and have chosen a viable career, there will always be jobs waiting for you. So, choose a career wisely.

1. Dress appropriately in business attire, even if it is for a blue-collar job. Suits for men and women. No flip-flops, sneakers, or hiking boots. Men wear a tie. Ladies wear a knee-length skirt or dress, or pant suit.

2. Bring an up-to-date, properly laid out and neatly printed re-sume to the interview. Make sure the resume is rewritten spe-cifically for this interview with the name of the company in the heading: Resume, John Smith, for the Position of XYZ at the XYZ Company. It should emphasize your work and educational experiences which relate directly to the position for which you are interviewing.

3. Never begin by telling the interviewer that you want the job. You do not know if you do or not until the interview is over. It may sound good at the beginning, but wait until the job is de-scribed to you.

A. Think about the questions you want answered well before you have to ask them. Do not ask too many questions, but make sure the one's you do ask are relevant.

B. Ask about what matters to you as an employee including: What will be your responsibilities? Who will be your supervisor? Who is his or her supervisor? Who can hire and fire you?

4. Be friendly and likeable. Smile often. Look the interviewer in the eye. Volunteer personal information only when necessary, and then only the minium you can get by with.

5. If the interviewer asks about your hobbies and outside interests, try and turn the question around to discover the interviewer's hobbies and interests. Then tailor your responses accordingly. Shared interests can help you get the job.

6. Establish yourself as someone memorable during the interview. Wear a brightly-colored but tasteful piece of clothing: scarf, tie, etc. Interviewers rarely remember people they have talked to by name, so make sure you stand out in their mind — the young woman with the red paisley scarf, the guy in the blue double-breasted jacket, etc.

Producer Danny Thomas hired Mary Tyler Moore for the Dick Van Dyke show because he recalled her smile from an interview a year or two before. That memorable smile helped make her a star

7. Research the company before the interview. What do they make and sell? What kind of research or product development do they do? What is their position in the market? Showing that you know something about the company tells the interviewer that you took the time to investigate and are not just shotgunning interviews.

8. Next, carefully read the job description for the position you are applying for. What in your work experience can you emphasize that fits what the company is looking for?

9. Never answer a question in the negative. If you are asked, did you supervise a department? Do not just say no. Instead say that you did not do so directly but you were responsible for leading others to accomplish specific tasks.

9. If the interviewer does not mention salary by the time the interview is ending, do not be afraid to bring it up yourself. If the offer is too low, say so and see if it can be raised. If not, decide if you want to continue. If not, politely tell the interviewer so, thank him or her for their time, and leave gracefully. Leaving with a good impression may result in a job interview in the future for a better position. One of the best jobs I ever had happened that way. I turned down a position in the initial interview but two months later was asked to interview for another, better job, which I accepted.

10. The interviewer will rarely provide enough information to answer all your questions. If this is a job you want, ask about specific aspects of the job. Say, "If I get the position, what specifically will be my repsonsibilities? Who are the other people in

the department or group and what are their skills? Do my skills fit what you are looking for? Tailor your responses to the answer. Final two questions, in this order: 1) what are the chances for advancement and 2) how are you judged for advancement?

11 As the interview comes to an end, you should have a feeling about how it has gone: 1) you will be considered, 2) you may be considered, 3) you will not be considered. No matter which, if you want the job, do or say something positive that will remain in the interviewer's mind, i.e., thank you for taking the time to talk with me. This appears to be a fine company and I would like to be a part of it.

12. The day after the interview, mail a typed, or better, a neatly handwritten letter to the interviewer (not an email) thanking them for their time, and reinforcing your interest. Include any details about your qualifications you may have forgotten, refer to something personal the interviewer said. Close by reemphasizing your interest in the position.

The Law

The law is something we take for granted. We even tend to ignore laws that we consider not very important or overreaching. That would be a mistake.

We are taught from an early age that laws are there to protect us. Only partially true. Laws are made by politicians and passed by committees and they serve three purposes which are, in descending order of importance: 1) more control over you by the government, 2) more power to the individual legislator or committee, and 3) solving a problem.

The less important the laws are and the smaller the groups of people they affect, the less scrutiny they get.

As an example of really bad law, recently, a California legislator rewrote and had passed a law that purported to protect people from buying counterfeit memorabilia. The law required that each autographed item have affixed to it a sworn, witnessed statement of the original owner's intent to sell. Sound reasonable?

Now for the unintended consequence.

Neither the legislator, the reviewing committees, nor the other legislators and senators who voted to approve it, nor the Govenor who signed it, considered all of its ramifications. For instance, is Michael Jordan going to sign an affidavit for a team shirt he gave away twenty years ago? Or is Albert Einstein going to come back from the grave to swear that he autographed and gave a book to a favorite student in 1938?

So little thought went into this law that no one in the legislature thought to be concerned about businesses beyond sports memorabilia which sold autographed books, photographs and art. When questioned by representatives of these dealers, the legislator blithely told them to ignore the law as it was not intended to include them. She knew so little about the legal process that it apparently did not occur to her that a judge hearing a case against a bookseller or art dealer might not see it that way. Nor did she think about the thousands of dollars that it would cost for that person to mount a defense in court.

The Constitution, and subsequent law, states that you are innocent until proven guilty. We know that government in the guise of a prosecuting attorney must prove you guilty.

But the prosecuting attorney has the full weight and economic support of government behind them. Add to that, the police who arrested you, and the prosecuting attorney trying your case do not care whether you are guilty or not. Your conviction is just another in the "win column," and another step to promotion.

So, break one of those minor or seemingly unimportant laws — and get caught doing so — and you will pay, and pay and pay.

And don't get me started on lawyers. All I can say is do everything in your power to avoid lawyers.

Marriage, and Other Relationships

Maintaining a marriage or other romantic relationship are among the most difficult tasks you will undertake. You promise to live with another person for the rest of your life. That means that you have to put up with all of their foibles and eccentricities — and they with yours — for years and years.

Respect your partner. Realize that many things you do will irritate them. Once you identify what they are, don't do them.

A marriage is a partnership, one that should be fifty-fifty in all things, from washing dishes to raising children.

Mutually carve out specific areas of responsibility. Hold up your end.

Don't rush into marriage or a romantic relationship. Look for real friendship. Sex should never be your main connection as the novelty and excitement eventually fades.

Money

One of the most important factors in your life is money. How to use it, how to save it, and how much to have when you lose a job or retire.

You should always keep in mind that a supply of money from a job is never assured. You can lose your position and salary for any of number of reasons over which you have no control. To surmount this problem, you must have sufficient savings, as discussed below, to ride out your period of unemployment.

And do not depend on the government to provide you with an unemployment check. They may do so, but it will never be enough to sustain you, particularly if you have a mortgage, rent, car payment(s) or a medical emergency.

Employment

One of the commonest reasons you may lose your job is a financial recession.

Since 1960 (56 years as this is written) there have been eight recessions that have thrown millions out of work. Several of those recessions were so severe that hundreds of thousands who lost their jobs were out of work so long that they considered themselves redundant and dropped out of the job market. Thousands more could not be rehired because their companies, and indeed, their entire industries, no longer existed.

Don't believe me — ask any of the thousands of workers in steel and auto industries who were let go over the past five decades. The steel industry nearly ceased to exist in the United States in the 1970s and '80s due to foreign competition, management's insistence on higher returns and union's refusal to recognize the dangers ahead of cheaper foreign competion. Their refusal to spend on modernization and research and development is a lesson that still has not been learned by far to many companies.

The auto industry imploded in the same period and into the 1990s due to poor management, terrible quality control and a refusal to modernize. Only in the last decade has the American auto industry recovered.

How bad was it? It used to be a truism in Detroit that if you worked for one of the Big Three automakers, you had a job for life. When the auto industry recovered and began to modernize, the manufacturing floors were populated with less than half the preimplosion employees. New technology in the form of automated processes, computers, and more efficient manufacturing techniques replaced thousands of workers. The loss of those thousands of jobs and their tax revenue, coupled with civic mismanagement of the highest order nearly turned the city of Detroit and much of the surrounding suburban area into a ghost town. Its total recovery is still iffy.

Credit Accounts

Excellent credit (750+ range in your credit report) is reached by paying off your credit card(s) and other bills every month. Before you make a credit purchase, consider whether or not you will be able to pay that bill, in addition to your other bills, every month.

If you cannot, do not make the purchase. Defer it until you can. Excellent credit will save you money in the long run as you will be offered lower financing rates when making large purchases such as a car, major appliance or a home.

Six Month Emergency Cushion

Keep at least six months – or more – cash in a savings account for emergency use. The amount should equal six months total salary, including taxes. "Emergency" should be defined as losing your job, watching your home burn down, a medical problem for you or someone close who needs help, an unexpected bill that must be paid like a car repair, plumbing problems, etc. An "emergency" is not a down payment on a new car or those expensive shoes, you just have to have, etc.

Retirement

At a young age (less than 30) retirement seems a "lifetime" away. You will be surprised at how fast it arrives.

Invest early (starting with your first job). Take advantage of the federal government's tax break investments like Individual Retirement Accounts (IRAs) and Roth IRAs. Save a certain amount in a retirement fund every month and by the time you retire you will be a millionaire. No kidding.

If you invest $12,000.00 per year between ages 23 and 67 at 6 to 10% average annual interest per year, you will have generated $1,820,000 dollars. This should be only one of your investments.

In 1921 my grandfather earned an annual salary of $1,100, less than $23 per week. He was married with two children.

In 1967 (46 years later), I made $10,000. A comfortable salary for a family of four. Our weekly family grocery bill for four was $27.00. Today it is $160.00 for two.

Today, 49 years later, I average nine times what I earned in 1967. So, assuming that rate of inflation averages 3%, a family of four will need $430,411 in 2062 to live a comfortable life.

One more example: during the early 1960s, a men's clothing company advertised suits in men's magazines under the Cricketeer brand name ". . . for the man who wants to make Ten Thousand dollars a year before he is thirty." That's poverty level today.

You are going to need a lot of money to retire comfortably. The younger you are when you start, the less you will have to save each month. A reputable investment counselor will advise you how to do so. You may want to find a licensed and bonded advisor, or one who represents either a series of mutual funds with a proven track record of returns over a twenty year period, or a for-fee adviser with the same type of track record.

Start as young as possible. Your bank's withholding plan can transfer a set amount from your paycheck or checking account every month to a mutual stock fund. If you use the withholding plan, you can adjust your spending to do without the money you are investing.

Again, I urge you to start as young as possible. As you grow older, you will have more and more expenses that will make it that much harder to save for retirement. In your thirties you will have car and house or rent payments and probably children to raise. In your forties, you will add home repairs, upgrades, and teenage children's expenses. In your fifties, you will add college educations and it will be almost impossible to save. In your sixties, it will be too late and you may have parental care expenses as well.

Another good way to invest — after starting your retirement fund — is in you. Start your own business. Find a niche in one of your hobbies, or your chosen profession and develop a product (book, instrument, gadget, etc.) to fill it. The benefits are three fold:

1) you will be earning extra money to invest, and

2) you will not have to argue with a boss about the right way to do something — because you will be the boss. This will become a most attractive proposition when you have worked in a job for a few years. And, it may turn out to be your main source of income and satisfaction. It has been for me.

Organization

Organizing your life should be driven by **long term goals** and **daily goals**.

Long term goals can be, and should be — where do I want to be in five years, ten years. Write these down somewhere where you can keep and review them periodically. Don't be afraid to change them as your circumstance's change. As you age, you will find your long term goals not only evolving but coming into sharper focus.

Short term goals are much easier to list and complete. My favorite short term goal list is a daily to-do list. I make it up at the end of the work day, listing the three to seven (never more) most important tasks I wish to accomplish the next day.

Doing it the night before does not waste any of my most productive time of the day, the first work hour in the morning. Don't just write "finish report." Add the name of the report and a few quick points you wish to incorporate. Don't write "appointment" write down who the appointment is with and what actions need to be discussed. Don't write, "birthday gift," write down who it is for and one or two suggestions.

By adding these notes to your tasks, your subconscious will be working overnight and you will find it easier to finish the report, get to an appointment on time, or think of the perfect birthday gift for that person.

Arrange the tasks or goals in priority of their importance. Obviously "finish a report for work" is more important than "car service" — unless your car is not running, in which case it may assume top priority if you need the car to get to work.

It is always a good idea to try and fit these daily goals in with your long term goals.

Every seemingly insolvable project or problem is composed of interdependent components. Identify each component, develop a plan to solve each, and then combine them. This will usually suggest a way to solve the overall problem.

I apply the following organizational technique to my writing and you can use it as well when writing reports, etc. Whether writing a novel or nonfiction book, I write two-three pages a day. I then put the new pages aside, edit and rewrite the pages I wrote the previous day. Repeating this process every day helps me keep in mind where I am in the narrative and reminds me of any changes I made to yesterday's copy. I can then start the next set of pages on track.

Personal Demeanor At Work

In interactions with others, this is quite important, particularly in business. The key is to always act as if you know exactly where you are going and what you are doing — even if you don't. If someone in authority looks at you, meet their gaze, eye-to-eye, with a slight smile. If they were intent on harassing you with a penny-ante task, as many in authority like to do, this usually changes their mind.

In meetings, don't sit like a bump on a log, even if you have nothing to contribute. Always bring a note pad and take notes. This will impress your superiors and show that you are paying attention. Don't doodle, take actual notes. Someone may want to see them. Carry that notepad with you as much as possible. It will make you seem busy, even when you are not.

When I worked for a certain company, there were four of us managing departments. We were all of the same age. One of us always carried a yellow tablet. He would take notes with a black felt-tipped pen and make lists of things to be done. I once asked him why he used a felt-tipped pen. He said so that his boss, and his bosses' boss would notice.

He became the president of that multimillion dollar company. He really did.

Politics and Politicians

Do not believe everything a politician says, ever.

A politician's first priority is to be elected. Second priority is to be reelected. All decisions a politician makes about the public welfare are based on his first two priorities. Anything accomplished for the public benefit is usually incidental to being elected or reelected.

All politicians, elected officials, and the very rich, know they are more equal, and more entitled than you. Ignore their objections to the contrary.

Machiavelli wisely said

"put not your trust in princes,"

meaning never trust a government or any of its employees for, like religions, they answer to a higher authority and this is their excuse for doing whatever they want.

"Democracy is the worst form of government,
except all others."

Winston Churchill

Privacy

Few things are more important than your personal privacy. Since the 1980s and the widespread use of computers to gather meta-data, our personal privacy has been breached. Government and commercial interests collect "data" on each of us. And it is rarely used to our benefit.

Commercial concerns and internet providers (Goggle, Yahoo, etc.) and social sites (Facebook and their ilk) assure us that the data is only gathered to serve us better by presenting information about products we might be interested in. Nonsense! Government claims that our personal data is collected to safeguard us from terrorists and other threats. It is the other threats that worry me — what are they and who decides they are a threat?

Commercial data can, and has been, used against us. Commercial interests (Google, Yahoo, Facebook, Twitter, etc.) sell the data they collect to the highest bidder and we are deluged with mail, both snail and electronic, for products for which we have little interest. Those same organizations use that data to track us from place to place and uncover the details of our private affairs.

That data is always for sale and we cannot even begin to imagine and prepare for the harm it might do us. Why would you want some faceless entity with billions of dollars at their disposal and thousands of people ready and willing to do their bidding to know where you are every minute of the day?

Since 9/11, the U.S. government has been tracking American citizens so closely that it would have made Heinrich Himmler, the head of Hitler's Nazi SS or Lavrentiy Beria, the head of Stalin's infamous NKVD in Soviet Russia, swoon with jealousy.

Can You Protect Yourself from Government and Commercial Snooping – No.

1) Nothing on the internet is private — no matter what claim is made to the contrary by anyone.

2) If you must use a social site such as Facebook, keep in mind that anything you put on Facebook will remain on the internet forever and will be available to anyone who cares to look. This is true even if you cancel your Facebook, Twitter, Snapchat, etc. accounts. Nowhere in their disclosures does it say that they will delete your information if you close your account. And in any event, that information will still be on the internet as it has been migrated to other web sites by people known or unknown to you, a process over which neither you nor Facebook — or any other social media — have control.

3) If you apply for a job, for college, military service, etc., your Facebook and other social media sites will be examined. If you have ever placed anything on your page about drinking, drunkenness, drugs, sex, or disparaging remarks about other people because of race, color, religion, etc., be assured that it will be discovered.

Some Ideas to Slow Down The Snoopers

1) Always use private or incognito pages to search the web. Even then, a concealed record of every site you visit is kept by the internet provider and this data is for sale.

2) Always set your internet options to "do not track," although it probably will not do any good.

3) Always use passwords of at least 8-14 characters long which are a mix of numbers, letters, and symbols. Change them at least every six months. Use a password manager such as Last Pass which will generate passwords and record them for you.

4) Keep a list of your passwords, but not on your computers, tablets or phones.

5) If you make a credit card purchase, use the credit card company's "one use credit card number service."

6) Once you graduate from college, close your Facebook account and open a new one with a new password. If you used a shortened version of your name or nickname to open your first account, use your full name — as you would list on a job or other application — to open the new one. This may provide some protection against anyone finding your old account.

You have no idea how what you posted between junior high and college graduation may be viewed, used and interpreted by another, including those in a position to hire or fire you.

Religion

I am not going to discuss religion in any depth. Like sex, it is something better learned without instruction.

Be aware that all religions, like governments, are run by bureau-cracies and, when push comes to shove, they will defend the organization and not the idea.

Whether or not you believe in one god, or a variety of gods, is your choice.

I make it a practice to never discuss religion with anyone, ever, especially a priest, minister, rabbi, mullah, guru, etc. Their job is to sell you on their brand of religion.

I am sure you can develop a better personal religion — if you need one — than the current mass religions which seem to be, or have been, preoccupied with shunning, proscribing or killing anyone who does not follow their beliefs to the letter, always in the name of their "god." Because "god" told them to do so, they are free to act with impunity whenever they proslytise or feel threatened

Rules to Live By

Don't take yourself to seriously, no one else does except your parents and siblings.

Pay your credit cards off every month.

Save for retirement beginning with your first pay check. Whatever you think you will need to retire on, double it, add 40% and you will only be half wrong.

When you want to do or be something in life, do not let anyone discourage you. What do they know? Just do it. A high school English teacher told me I would never become an author.

Whatever bad happens to you, just think of this: in five years, how much will this matter?

When you just have to buy something you do not really need, think of this: in a week or so, will I say to myself, what did I buy that for?

Whether you are a parent or not, make every child's growing years memorable.

Science

Science is based on fact and not emotion. Emotion does not require critical thinking, science does.

Scientific discoveries are made this way:

> Hypothesis: I think this might work . . .

> Fact gathering: do your research and double check whatever you learn . . .

> Theory: my research leads me to believe that it works this way . . .

> Proof: I have tested my theory and can find no other way it might work . . .

Apply this mind-set to your everyday life and you can't go too far wrong.

Beware of charlatans who use science to persuade you to a course of action. Demand the proof behind their views and examine it with a critical eye. Like crooked politicians, there are many scientific charlatans out there.

Skill Sets You Must Have

Every man or woman should be able to:

1. Cook a meal
2. Make a bed
3. Clean a house
4. Drive a car
5. Play at least one musical instrument, however badly
6. Shoot a rifle, pistol and shotgun accurately at 25 yards.
7. Be able to defend yourself with your fists and feet, or a club — remember that an attacker can run at you from a distance of 8-10 feet faster than you can draw a gun, knife or set yourself to meet the attack. Always keep a threat at least twelve to eighteen feet distant.

(Remember this the next time you read or hear a derogatory media report about a cop shooting a suspect armed with a knife.)

Climate Change

I saved this section for last because I think it will be more important than anything else in your lives. Climate change is causing, and will continue to cause, changes in the way you live — and most will be negative. You have probably heard about climate change for so long that it has become a constant background drone to which you pay little attention. After you read the following paragraphs, I hope it will prompt you to pay more attention, do your own research, and make preparations.

The planet's climate is changing and getting warmer; there is no longer any doubt about it. The glaciers are melting faster than at any time in the past ten thousand years. Sea levels are rising at unprecedented rates. Weather is growing hotter and more humid. Here in California scientists have estimated that 110 million trees are dead or dying due to increased heat which has caused infestations by insects and massive forest fires. We could lose a large percentage of western forests by the turn of this century.

Reservoirs throughout the Southwest are at historical lows; they store your drinking water. It will take years of normal rainfalls to refill them. And there is little possibility of the rainy seasons we knew in the first seven decades of the 20th century returning.

This means that the way you live over the next eighty-plus years will change dramatically.

Food prices will rise as growers abandon our current California farm lands because of lack of water and increasing desertification. New farming methods will develop but they will all involve additional costs leading to higher food prices.

Populations will migrate to the cities once more as the distribution of water and food becomes more centralized.

Electrical power will be rationed as summer heat and winter cold increases. By 2060, late summer temperatures in the Midwestern and Southern States could routinely reach 110-120 F for weeks at a time. Fossil fuel use will decline by government fiat, but it is problematical if non-fossil fuels sources will be able to meet the increased demand. Carbon levels are already so high that climate change effects will persist well beyond your lifetimes.

As sea levels rise, coastal cities may disappear either wholly or partially. The economic repercussions will be enormous.

Storms of all types will become more severe and deadly. In 1950, severe climate-induced storms averaged two per year world-wide. By 2007, the average had risen to six. Imagine what the average number will be in 2060, only forty-four years away as this is written.

Emigration from equatorial regions will grow as a result of rising temperatures, severe storms, increasing poverty, civil disorder, and criminality. The United States will remain a prime destination for all legal and illegal immigrants.

The United States, as well as the rest of the world, will see increasing criminality due to dissatisfaction as the government fails to deal effectively with the effects of climate change. Political factions (both conservative and liberal) will become increasingly radicalized. Homegrown terrorism will rise as a result of political radicalism, opportunistic criminals, and the widening gap between the rich and poor. The middle class will continue to decline.

Climate change will effect your health and well-being via rising stress levels, exposure to prolonged summer heat and winter cold, and exploding populations of disease-carrying insects and rodents. In 2003, 70,000 people in Europe died during summer heat waves due to cardiac stress and respiratory causes. Most of Europe north of the Alps used to experience mild summers with temperatures rarely reaching 90 F. France experienced eight days of 104 F temperatures during the 2002 heat wave and 14,802 deaths resulted. Before 1990, Most northern European countries experienced one mild heat wave every eight years; since 2006 the average has risen to one every year. Heat waves also destroy many food crops.

This is the world that you will live in as you grow older. The changes I have seen since the 1940s, not in technology, but in the growth of the nation's population (139.5 million in the year I was born, 1939, vs. 318.9 million in 2014), deepening poverty levels, loss of blue collar jobs in all areas of work, increasing cost of food, electricity and other necessities, declines in the middle class, gross increases in government bureaucracies at all levels, political polarization, growth of youth gangs, accelerating drug use, will only continue.

When I was a teenager, homelessness was almost unknown. Today it is at epidemic proportions. What will it be like ten, twenty, thirty years from now?

You must be aware of these changes or they may swamp you as they already have done to millions of Americans.

Plan for these changes. Think about how you can take advantage of them not only to protect yourself and your future families, but how you can use them to maintain and even improve your lives as you age.

-30-

Good luck to the five of you. This booklet is by no means a guide to how to live your life. Rather, consider it as a compilation of lessons I have learned the hard way. I hope they might help smooth the bumps in your lives. Good luck and live a long, happy, and healthy life!

"Grandpa" Joe Poyer
November, 2016

1957

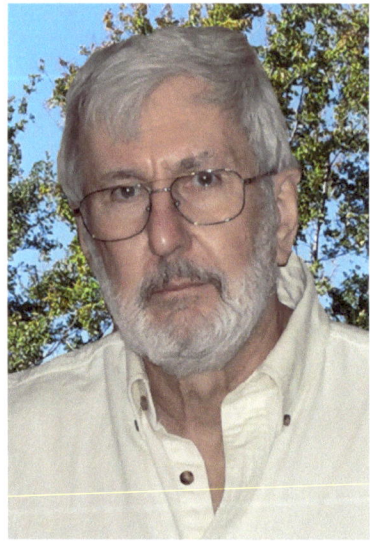

2016

www.ingramcontent.com/pod-product-compliance
Lightning Source LLC
Chambersburg PA
CBHW041802040426
42448CB00001B/12